ANIMAL PREDATORS

Owls

SANDRA MARKLE

CAROLRHODA BOOKS, INC./ MINNEAPOLIS

The Animal World Is Full of
PREDATORS.

Predators are the hunters who find, catch, and eat other animals—their prey—in order to survive. Every environment has its chain of hunters. The smaller, slower, less able predators become prey for the bigger, faster, more cunning hunters. And everywhere, there are just a few kinds of predators at the top of the food chain.

In nearly every habitat, this group of predators includes one or more kinds of owls, like this screech owl.

So why are owls, like this great gray owl, such great hunters? For one thing, they can swoop through the air nearly silently to strike with sharp talons (claws) and beak. Most owls hunt at night. To help them see, they have bigger eyes than most birds. Their big eyes face forward so they can judge how far to fly to catch prey. Their eyes also have powerful magnifying lenses so they can spot small prey over long distances. The pupils of their eyes (the openings at the center) can open super wide to let in more light when it is dark.

For protection and support, an owl's big eyes are inside bony tubes. But these tubes limit how much its eyes can move. To look left, right, up, or down, owls—like this northern saw-whet—must turn their heads. All owls' necks have lots of bones—nearly twice as many as a human's neck. These bones let the owl turn its head far enough to look almost straight behind itself.

An owl's disk-shaped face, like this barn owl's face, works like a satellite dish to collect sound waves. Under the feathers are huge ear openings. One is usually larger and lower on the owl's head than the other. This difference in size and position helps the owl quickly figure out where sounds are coming from.

The female great gray's feathers blend perfectly with the tree bark. While she rests, her big yellow eyes are half-closed and hidden by feather-covered lids. But then she hears a gopher's rustling noise. Her eyes snap wide open, and she studies the shadowy ground.

The instant a pocket gopher runs into the open, the great gray owl launches into flight. The great gray is among the world's biggest owls. The female's body is about 30 inches (80 centimeters) tall, and her wings stretch nearly 5 feet (about 1.5 meters) from tip to tip. Her big size makes her a powerful predator. She is able to kill bigger prey, such as rabbits and squirrels, that smaller owls couldn't catch. But her big size also means it takes more energy to fly. So the great gray prefers to hunt by perching and waiting. When prey comes within range, she drops off the branch, spreads her wings to slow her plunge, and swoops down.

This time, the big owl will need to fly a short distance to overtake her prey.   She does this nearly silently.   The front edges of most birds' wings are solid, like stiff fingers pressed together.   Such wings smack against the air with a thump. The leading edges of the owl's wings are fringed and flexible, like rubbery fingers spread apart. The upper surface of each feather also has a velvet coat of tiny strands. The great gray's wings slip through the air with the softest swish. When the female great gray is nearly over the gopher, she pulls in her wings and dives to attack.

The owl's fourth toe is turned backward to work like a thumb. She grabs the pocket gopher with one foot.

Next, the great gray uses another weapon—her sharp beak. A bristly feather mustache around her beak lets her feel when she's close enough to bite her prey. Then she quickly kills it.

The great gray's wings provide enough lifting power to fly while carrying prey. So she flies back to her favorite perch. There, high above the forest floor, she can eat, safe from ground-hunting predators like foxes, who might try to steal her meal. No longer out in the open, she is also less likely to have to defend her food from flying predators, such as hawks and other owls.

Like this pygmy owl, all owls have wide mouths. Whenever possible, they swallow their prey in one gulp. But if the meal is really big, the owl will rip off chunks.

Next, digestive juices in the owl's stomach go to work. But the digestive juices can't break down the prey's teeth, fur, and bones. The food passes from the stomach into a muscular sac called the gizzard. There, the broken-down food is turned into a soft mass and passed on into the intestine to finish being digested.

The bits left in the gizzard are squeezed and packed together. Then the owl throws up a soft pellet of these wastes. When an owl perches in the same spot day after day, the leafy forest floor below becomes littered with these pellets.

An owl needs to fly in order to catch food. So when it isn't flying, the owl spends a lot of time preening, or caring for its feathers. This burrowing owl carefully pulls each of its outer feathers through its beak.

Feathers are made up of hundreds of strands held together by tiny hooks. Flying or struggling with prey can separate the feather strands. All owls, including this screech owl, have to preen regularly to fasten their feathers together again.

The feathers of an owl's coat match its surroundings. This helps it hide wherever it waits to ambush (surprise) prey. The Arctic region has few trees and a lot snow much of the year. The snowy owl's coloring lets it hide in plain sight in the Arctic while sitting on the ground.

This male snowy owl was waiting next to the entrance to a lemming's tunnel. When the lemming started running, the snowy owl was only a hop away. He'll deliver this meal to his mate.

This male barn owl is delivering a meal too. It's a gift to win a mate. Most owls start nesting in late winter. The female will need to spend about one month sitting on her eggs. This will keep them warm while the babies grow inside the eggs. The male's food gift shows he can be counted on to do all of the hunting during this time.

Whoo, hoo-hoo-hoo. Whoo, hoo-hoo-hoo. This male great horned owl flies from perch to perch. At each stop, he hoots loudly to tell other great horned males to stay away from his home range. This range, often a large area, is where he'll hunt to feed his mate and offspring.

Female owls lay their eggs as long as four days apart. The first chicks to hatch may be two weeks older than the youngest ones. At first, the chicks' eyes are closed and their feathers are thin. This mother great gray owl keeps the chicks close to her warm body. When it rains, she holds her wings open over them like a feather-covered umbrella.

When a hawk circles overhead, looking for a meal, the mother great gray owl fluffs up her feathers to look bigger. When the hawk swoops closer, the mother owl hisses and clicks her beak noisily. This threat works, and the hawk flies away. While the mother owl stays with her young family, the father owl keeps on hunting.

At first, owl chicks, or owlets, are too small to swallow prey whole. The female screech owl tears off small, boneless, featherless bits of the food the male brings to her. Then, closing her eyes to protect them from the chick's beak, she feeds the bits to her offspring. This food will be easier for the chick to digest because it doesn't contain any wastes to cough up.

When the chick is full, it goes back into its nest. This nest is a natural hole in the tree. Most owls don't build nests. Sometimes they take over the abandoned nest of a hawk or a crow. More often, they find a cavity (hole) in a tree or use a broken-off treetop for a nest. Owls don't even add any nesting material. The eggs and the young rest directly on the wood chips or other matter that are already on the floor of the cavity.

The female snowy owl's nest is just a dip in the ground. Like the screech owl, the mother snowy owl tears off bits of meat for her babies. She starts by feeding the chicks begging most actively. Those are usually the older, bigger chicks. So if the meal isn't very big, the smaller chicks get less to eat. And if food becomes scarce, the younger chicks may die. They may even become food for the older chicks. That way, at least some of the owlets survive.

of time and energy hunting to provide food for the growing owlets.

Eventually, growing owlets get so big that both parents must hunt to keep their hungry offspring fed. Left on their own, these young screech owls huddle together to keep warm and safe. Side by side, the three little owlets look much bigger and are less likely to be attacked by any hungry hawks or other owls flying overhead.

The wings of these ten-week-old horned owls are not yet strong enough for flight. But that doesn't stop the owlets from exploring by walking along the branches. When one owlet starts to fall, he grabs on with his toes. Then he uses his beak to pull himself up onto the branch again.

This young screech owl is strong and practiced enough to fly. But its hunting skills are weak. With practice, the youngster quickly learns to catch easy prey, like a hornworm.

When this young female saw-whet owl first tried to catch a mouse, the mouse escaped. Hunger forced the young female to keep practicing. Like all owls, the young saw-whet was naturally equipped to be a good hunter. Her coloring let her blend in to hide in treetops while she watched for prey. Her excellent hearing and eyesight let her detect and pinpoint prey even in poor light. Her fringed feathers let her fly nearly silently to surprise prey. The young owl only has to perfect the timing of her attack.

Finally, the female saw-whet is successful. As she grabs the mouse, the young owl becomes part of a new generation of hunters on the wing.

Looking Back

- Look at the flying screech owl on page 20. Why does it have its wing tips spread apart? You'll find a clue on page 9.

- Look again at the owls' eyes in this book. Imagine how big your eyes would be if they were that large compared to the rest of your head.

- Look back at page 28. Why do you think the hole in the tree was a good place for the owl's nest?

- Look at the owl's feet on page 6. How are the owl's feet like your hands? How are they different?

Glossary

CHICK: a baby bird

EGG: the hard-shelled structure in which a baby bird develops

FEATHER: a protective body covering of birds. Tiny hooks hold the many strands of wing feathers together.

GIZZARD: the muscular body part that helps birds break down the food they eat

PELLET: a compacted ball of waste, including bones, teeth, and fur, that an owl throws up

PREDATOR: an animal that is a hunter

PREENING: the process by which a bird pulls feathers through its beak to fasten separated feather strands together again

PREY: an animal that a predator catches to eat

PUPIL: the opening of the eyeball that lets light enter the eye

STOMACH: a body part that stores and begins to break down food

TALONS: a bird's claws

WING: a body part that lifts a bird and moves it forward in flight

Further Information

Books

Arnosky, Jim. *All about Owls.* New York: Scholastic, 1999. This book investigates the biology and behavior of the owls of North America, with a special focus on the great horned owl.

Biel, Timothy. *Owls.* San Diego: Zoobooks, 2001. Striking photography illustrates this guide to amazing facts about owls.

Epple, Wolfgang. *Barn Owls.* Photographs by Manfred Rogl. Minneapolis: Carolrhoda Books, Inc., 1992. Author and photographer team up for an up close look at a barn owl's life history.

Sattler, Helen Roney. *Owls on Silent Wings.* Niwot, CO: Roberts Rinehart Publishing, 1999. This book includes the biology and behavior of owls, plus Native American legends about these amazing birds.

Tagholm, Sally. *Barn Owl.* New York: Larousse Kingfisher Chambers, 2003. This book offers a detailed look at the life of a barn owl.

Videos

Amazing Birds of America (Questar, Inc., 1999). This video contains footage of 150 species of birds, including the great horned owl.

Owls Up Close (Ark Media Group, Ltd., 1992). This film explores the lives and behaviors of different kinds of owls.

Index

With love for good friends Terry and Kath Mundy

The author would like to thank Irina Menyushina, research scientist for Wrangel Island State Nature Reserve, for sharing her expertise and enthusiasm, and especially for her many years studying snowy owls in the wild. And a very special thanks to Skip Jeffery for his help and support.

Photo Acknowledgments

The images in this book are used with the permission of: © ABPL/Lanz Von Horsten/Animals Animals, p. 1; © Joe McDonald/CORBIS, pp. 3, 13, 20, 33, 35; © Erwin and Peggy Bauer, pp. 4, 7; © Maslowski Photo, pp. 5, 8, 21, 22, 23, 24, 28, 31; © W. Perry Conway/CORBIS, p. 6; © Daniel J. Cox/naturalexposures.com, p. 11; © Michael Quinton, pp. 12, 14, 27, 34; © Claus Meyer/Minden Pictures, p. 17; © John Hoffman/Bruce Coleman, Inc., p. 18; © Phyllis Greenberg/Animals Animals, p. 19; © Gary R. Jones/Bruce Coleman, Inc., p. 26; © Andy Harmer, p. 32; © Dwight R. Kuhn, p. 36.
Cover: © Stephen Dalton/Animals Animals. Back cover: © Maslowski Photo.

Carolrhoda Books, Inc.
A division of Lerner Publishing Group
241 First Avenue North
Minneapolis, MN 55401 U.S.A.

Website address: www.lernerbooks.com

Library of Congress Cataloging-in-Publication Data

Markle, Sandra.
    Owls / by Sandra Markle.
       p.   cm.—(Animal predators)
    Summary: Discusses the physical characteristics of owls that combine to make them such able predators.
    Includes bibliographical references (p.) and index.
    ISBN: 1–57505–729–8 (lib. bdg. : alk. paper)
    1. Owls—Juvenile literature. [1. Owls.] I. Title. II. Series.
    QL696.S8M257 2004
    598.9'7—dc22   2003023019

Manufactured in the United States of America
1 2 3 4 5 6 – DP – 09 08 07 06 05 04